PECULIAR PETS

Words Of Imagination

Edited By Sarah Waterhouse

First published in Great Britain in 2021 by:

Young Writers
Remus House
Coltsfoot Drive
Peterborough
PE2 9BF
Telephone: 01733 890066
Website: www.youngwriters.co.uk

Printed and bound in the UK by BookPrintingUK
Website: www.bookprintinguk.com
YB0456I

★ FOREWORD ★

Welcome Reader!

Are you ready to discover weird and wonderful creatures that you'd never even dreamed of?

For Young Writers' latest competition we asked primary school pupils to create a Peculiar Pet of their own invention, and then write a poem about it! They rose to the challenge magnificently and the result is this fantastic collection full of creepy critters and amazing animals!

Here at Young Writers our aim is to encourage creativity in children and to inspire a love of the written word, so it's great to get such an amazing response, with some absolutely fantastic poems. Not only have these young authors created imaginative and inventive animals, they've also crafted wonderful poems to showcase their creations and their writing ability. These poems are brimming with inspiration. The slimiest slitherers, the creepiest crawlers and furriest friends are all brought to life in these pages – you can decide for yourself which ones you'd like as a pet!

I'd like to congratulate all the young authors in this anthology, I hope this inspires them to continue with their creative writing.

★ CONTENTS ★

ACS Cobham International School, Hersham

Layla Hassan (7)	1
Emma Barnett (7)	2
Ryder Fox (7)	4
Hasti Brannigan (8)	6
Gabriel Morrar (7)	7
Maya Eva E Hosein (7)	8
Bella Ford (7)	9
Luke Storrer (7)	10
Isabella X (6)	11
Owen Jonk (7)	12
Mor Ben Shai (6)	13
Alice Gouvea Haberli (7)	14
Henry Hawkins (6)	15
Michelle Chen (7)	16
Aidan Ream (6)	17
Finn McVey	18
Jack Smithmier (7)	19
Ellie Kyrychenko (6)	20
Emily Hoy (6)	21
Nicolas Soler (8)	22
Isla Hamilton (5)	23
Suvi Sidhu (6)	24
Martina Azpilicueta (6)	25
Connor Custard (7)	26
Anna Ford (6)	27
Riad Rahmanov (6)	28
Harrison Doherty (6)	29
Bibi Merralls	30
Anian Enders (6)	31
Duke Storrer (7)	32

Alver Valley Schools, Rowner

Isabelle Milton-Leyshon (9)	33
Cassie Stuart (8)	34
George Aston Blanchard (7)	35
Kyle Blackman (8)	36
Riley Coatsworth (8)	37
Blair Hutton (8)	38
Lacey Oakes (8)	39
Benjamin Britten (8)	40
Eric Gomes (9)	41
Ailish Richards (8)	42
Darcie Smith (8)	43
Lily Hall (9)	44
William François Frost (9)	45
Ruby Pitfield (8)	46
Madison Walker (8)	47
Lillie Jade Buchanan (8)	48
Aiden McAllister (8)	49
Karley Morgan (8)	50
Elsie Smethest (8)	51
Laila-Mae Lavin (8)	52
Layton Duruy (8)	53
Scarlett Hedger (8)	54
Reggie Peart (8)	55
Beay Edwards (9)	56
Amelie Langan (8)	57
Lilliana Nelson (9)	58
Joseph Feeley (8)	59
Noah Styan (8)	60
Lucy Francis (8)	61
Marcus Kwabena Mprah (8)	62
Ben Kershaw (8)	63
Raluca Segarceanu (8)	64
Harvey Matthews (8)	65
Harrison Pearce (8)	66

Ila Kaminski (8)	67
Max Butler (8)	68
Harley Allen (9)	69
George Grimes (8)	70
Penelope Hearn (8)	71
Edward Harvey (9)	72
Archie Farrel (8)	73

Newton Bluecoat CE Primary School, Newton With Scales

Georgie Short (8)	74
Isla Bradley (8)	76
Bobby Hastwell (8)	78
Isaac Wearden (8)	79
Jude Westgate (8)	80
Millie Singleton (8)	81
Logan Salisbury (8)	82
Lyla Fegan (8)	83
Paige Hulme (8)	84
Harriet Cross (8)	85
Alfie Jones (8)	86
Ben Bayley (8)	87
Amelia Cole (9)	88
Alijah Davidson (8)	89
Xzavier Whitehead (8)	90
Zak Tabbenor (9)	91
Joshua Baugh (8)	92
Scott Simpson (8)	93

St Joseph's & St Gregory's Catholic Primary School, Biddenham

Shyloh Gould (7)	94
Aleeza Hayat (7)	95
Anna Olutimayin (6)	96
Michael Udoh (6)	97
Apio Okel (8)	98
Jake Palmer (6)	99
Aradhana James (8)	100
Mason Grygiel-Smith (6)	101
Jihan Alom (6)	102
Mahdiya Bi (7)	103

Breann D'souza (6)	104
Grazi Alexandre Cardoso (7)	105
Marcel Popko (7)	106
Arman Chimber (8)	107
Aaminah Khan (7)	108
Vilte Zubaviciute (6)	109
Mujtabah Shahab (7)	110
Enzo Bucolo (7)	111
Hafsa Mahmood (7)	112
Imogen Waruhari (6)	113
Rameesha Begum (6)	114
Nihal Gill (6)	115
Achan Okel (8)	116
Ellis Matarazzo (7)	117
Nimrah Iqbal (7)	118
Manha Farheen (6)	119
Rizwan Waheed (7)	120

St Palladius Primary School, Dalry

Deja Parker (10)	121
Emma Galloway (11)	122
Skye McDowall (11)	124
Lucy Allan (11)	126
Ivie James Sharp (10)	128
Caoilin O'Reilly (9)	129
Cameron Irvine (10)	130
Kahlan Parker (10)	131
Hayden McKerrell (8)	132
Robert O'Pray (11)	133
Archie Eagleson (8)	134
AJ Logan (9)	135
Cole Barclay (10)	136
Dale McCann (10)	137
Hannah Krishnamuthe (10)	138
Lucy McCallum (11)	139
Andrew Fraser (9)	140
Maisy Berrie (9)	141
Jodie Thompson (8)	142
Max Livingstone (9)	143
Riley Doak Winton (9)	144
Alan Billy Lee Harkins (10)	145
Grace Wright (9)	146
Danielle Kilday (11)	147

Destiny Allan (11)   148
Tilly Murdoch (9)   149

THE POEMS

COME ON SLOW COACH

Sparkle Sprite Shines So Bright

Sparkle Sprite shines so bright,
Under the stars and the moonlight.
She is cute, kind and clever
And she always makes things better.
She is incredibly extraordinary
And her white long paws are so furry.
She lives in the evergreen Bamboo Hotel
With her lovely family and friends, feeling all well.
She likes to go on walks to the Bamboo Store,
Where she eats some bamboo but she always
wants more.
She enjoys a marvellous and sunny day,
As all her worries go away.
She is gentle and caring with all her tiny friends
And their friendship never ends.
I wish, one day, we all can be
The best for Sparkle Sprite we can see.

Layla Hassan (7)
ACS Cobham International School, Hersham

Magical Unicorn

My pet is a unicorn,
Strong and magical.
My pet can fly.
It can do tricks in the sky.
She has a rainbow mane.
She is trained.
She is beautiful.
My pet is fourteen years old.
My pet is nice and kind.
My pet is helpful,
My pet loves helping people.
She helps people a lot,
Because she is a Helping Unicorn.
My pet is amazing.
I love my pet,
She is special.
My pet is great and powerful.
I love my pet
No matter what.
My pet has its own stuff
So I can tack her myself.

I don't need help with the tacking.
My pet is helpful,
She's nice, kind, great, powerful
And amazing.
I hope you will love my pet as much as I do!

Emma Barnett (7)
ACS Cobham International School, Hersham

The Rhyming Friends

Once upon a time,
There lived a dog called Leck.
He had a long neck.
He was such a wreck
He had a water bottle
The water bottle started to leak.
He was in such a freak!
Then he made such a great big shriek.
He wanted his friend Frog
And he lived in a bog.
Leck walked on a log
To get to Frog.
Then Leck walked on
He came to a tower.
He smelled a flower.
Then he took a shower.
Now it was time for bed,
He wanted to play with his toy car
Then he spotted a star
It looked far.

Time for bed, Leck,
Curl up your neck.

Ryder Fox (7)
ACS Cobham International School, Hersham

Black Bat

My big bat Goay
Is going to be fat and doughy.
He is friendly and funny
He goes to school with his friend Bunny.

His herd is kind
And his teachers are even kinder.
I wish to have a real pet
But now a pretend pet is my friend.

Hasti Brannigan (8)
ACS Cobham International School, Hersham

Buffalo

My buffalo is kind
It eats grass
It is a mammal
It is helpful
It has horns
If it gets scared, it charges
The buffalo lives in Botswana in Africa
It can live in deserts
It can live in Kenya in Africa
It is not a meat-eater.

Gabriel Morrar (7)
ACS Cobham International School, Hersham

Rithem

Rithem is so kind.
Rithem is so sweet.
I love Rithem
'Cause she doesn't tweet.
Rithem likes to bang
Rithem likes to boom
And Rithem likes to splash
All over Mr Bloom!
Rithem is my turtle
As sweet as can be.

Maya Eva E Hosein (7)
ACS Cobham International School, Hersham

Ealacorn

Deep under the water
Where there are only two sharks
Ealacorn and me swim deeper and deeper
Suddenly, an alarm goes
We boost up to the sky
Ealy and me
Me and Ealy
Together, we are perfect.

Bella Ford (7)
ACS Cobham International School, Hersham

The Intelligent Pet

I went to the movies
My pet ate other people's popcorn
And they got mad!
So we could not watch the movie
Me and my pet walked through the wall
And we did not get caught.

Luke Storrer (7)
ACS Cobham International School, Hersham

Pizza

My dog is scary but funny
She's only friendly to me

We went to the ice cream shop
When I walked in,
She was running to the ice cream
And ate it all!

Isabella X (6)
ACS Cobham International School, Hersham

Dino Do

My Dino Do always comes out at night
He calls when it's time to play
No one sees him
If anyone sees him, he hides
It's weird
Run away if you see him!

Owen Jonk (7)
ACS Cobham International School, Hersham

My Peculiar Pet

This is my unicorn
And we love each other.
She is the best pet
In the world
How I love cats and rabbits too.
My unicorn's name is Milly.

Mor Ben Shai (6)
ACS Cobham International School, Hersham

My Bunny Snowball

My bunny is funny
My bunny's favourite food is honey
Bang, crash, thump!
Snowball hit the wall
Snowball is as funny as a bunny!

Alice Gouvea Haberli (7)
ACS Cobham International School, Hersham

My Peculiar Pet

I took a walk
On the way, I met my friend called Aidan
And my frog
But then the frog threw me in the river
Then we had a swim with him.

Henry Hawkins (6)
ACS Cobham International School, Hersham

The Two Rabbits

Two girls.
They eat orange carrots.
The rabbits jump!
They live in a house in China.
One's name is An An.

Michelle Chen (7)
ACS Cobham International School, Hersham

The Rhyming Bird

Tom is a rhyming bird
And he is a making bird
Tom is a falling bird
But I say, "You have to stay home."

Aidan Ream (6)
ACS Cobham International School, Hersham

My Peculiar Pet

You think of getting a dog
You want to call it Cookie
I went with it to the movies
But he ate all the candy!

Finn McVey
ACS Cobham International School, Hersham

Peculiar Pets

Rock and Fly
And Claw and me
Went to a movie
When we went out of the movies
My pets went crazy!

Jack Smithmier (7)
ACS Cobham International School, Hersham

Rosie

She can jump.
She can run.
She can climb.
She can do magic.
She is so lucky.
She is so smart.

Ellie Kyrychenko (6)
ACS Cobham International School, Hersham

My Catacorn

My Catacorn is fabulous
At daytime, it's awake
At night-time, it's asleep
And it's rainbow.

Emily Hoy (6)
ACS Cobham International School, Hersham

My Dog

I once had a dog
Who looked like a frog
He liked to bounce around
But couldn't ride a log.

Nicolas Soler (8)
ACS Cobham International School, Hersham

Peculiar Pets

Dogcorn and I played in the yard
A fox came over
The fox followed the Dogcorn
Around the yard.

Isla Hamilton (5)

ACS Cobham International School, Hersham

My Peculiar Pet

Me and Felix were silly and funny
As funny as you
He would come to me at night
He would fart!

Suvi Sidhu (6)
ACS Cobham International School, Hersham

Ocker

The dog called Ocker is funny
Because he's funny, I love him
He is adorable
I love him.

Martina Azpilicueta (6)
ACS Cobham International School, Hersham

Dragon In The Sky

I have a dragon
My dragon's name is Lightning
It zooms through the sky
Like lightning.

Connor Custard (7)
ACS Cobham International School, Hersham

She Likes To Play

My pet is Uni
She does a unicycle
And sleeps
She likes to play
And peek.

Anna Ford (6)
ACS Cobham International School, Hersham

Porky

My caterpillar is very
Hungry and scary
And stinky
And very sleepy!

Riad Rahmanov (6)
ACS Cobham International School, Hersham

Turtle

Super Turtle fights crime
And after a good day
He says, "Hooray!"

Harrison Doherty (6)
ACS Cobham International School, Hersham

Peculiar Pets

Some puppies and dogs like food
Some like toys
Some wear sunglasses!

Bibi Merralls
ACS Cobham International School, Hersham

This Is My Fun Bat Poem

This is my bat
You might notice
He's a little flat!

Anian Enders (6)

ACS Cobham International School, Hersham

Danny Duke

He is clever
He can climb and fly
He is Danny Duke.

Duke Storrer (7)
ACS Cobham International School, Hersham

All About Stripy Spot!

S tripy and spotty, she's very happy

T ogether, we work as a team

R eally tall and kind, but very fierce and mean

I know when I'm ill I can count on her to make me feel better

P ouncing about, she makes me beam

Y es, she loves everyone and makes everyone smile as happy as can be

S oon she's sleepy like a koala and everyone goes away because they want more

P eople start leaving, except me because I take her home

O nce we're home, we snuggle up in bed, watching TV

T hen we fall asleep together nicely and happily and quietly.

Isabelle Milton-Leyshon (9)
Alver Valley Schools, Rowner

Moon And The Bone

M oon is cool, but not that cool
O i! Moon is actually a troublemaker
O h Moon, stop right now!
N o, I hate it when she plays up

M y pet is cool
O h yes she is
O h yes, she howls, oh no!
N ow she howls

M oon has powers she likes
O i, you! Have you heard she's a bit grumpy?
O h, Moon wants to be a hero
N ot much of a hero, but my hero!

M oon likes to howl
O h moon, why'd you do it?
O i! She can't leave in the day
N o, no! I can't hear her...

Cassie Stuart (8)
Alver Valley Schools, Rowner

Sinister Boatshark

B oatshark is a special shark for killing

O ptimistic when there are people, so he can eat them

A t the beach, you might be terrified because my shark bites you!

T onight, he looks for his precious prey in the water

S harp teeth as sharp as a knife, so watch out

H a to the people, from the sharp, shiny, sinister shark

A s my shark kills, you should run away

R un away to Africa if you don't want to see this sinister shark!

K angaroos are the sharp, sinister shark's rival.

George Aston Blanchard (7)
Alver Valley Schools, Rowner

Vegetarian Dog

V egetarian food is very delicious
E xcellent vegetables, very fresh every day
G iant dogs love to eat fresh grapes
E very day dogs love to eat fresh veg
T oo beautiful to say no to
A lot of hairs on its back
R eally helpful all the time
I ntelligent dog all the time
A lways overeating all the time
N aughty dog chasing people

D oes as it's told always
O verjoyed all the time
G ood as gold.

Kyle Blackman (8)
Alver Valley Schools, Rowner

Bungee-Jumping Chickmunk

Chickmunk likes to fly high
In the beautiful blue skies.
He likes to put up a fight
But watch out, he might bite.
Chickmunk is as small as an ant
But as violent as an angry tiger
He will fight
Until night
But when he sleeps, he leaps out of bed
Because there is a giant storm.
Chickmunk is unique underground
Doesn't need a pound
Is as loud as a hound.
He is as muddy as a big pig
And as playful as a puppy.
He is fierce and brave
Might not behave.

Riley Coatsworth (8)
Alver Valley Schools, Rowner

Cyborg Squirrel's Revenge

C ountlessly saves lives
Y ears of being alone, being bullied
B attling bad guys
O n his tree, there is crime
R ides on a robot rodent
G oes on adventures when he has the time

S aves civilians from criminals.
Q ueues up for acorns at the store
U nseen like a shadow
I n the shadows
R eally cool like the galaxy
R eally heroic
E ats nuts and bolts
L ives unseen.

Blair Hutton (8)
Alver Valley Schools, Rowner

Giraffe Fly

G reat friend to help you with learning

I ncredible swimmer in a race

R eally amazing singer for you

A mazing buddy for when you're sad

F antastic cook for when you're hungry

F abulous designer to make you look nice

E xtremely long neck like an elephant trunk.

F ast runner for when you're tired

L ovely singer to make you music

Y apping and yellow like the golden sun.

Lacey Oakes (8)

Alver Valley Schools, Rowner

My Pet Thangbatfrog

T he last Batfrog in existence.
H unting all the evil souls
A s fierce as a tiger.
N orth is where it was born.
G reater than the world.
B rave for a pet, it's like a ninja.
A Batfrog I call him.
T errible at dancing.
F antastic like flickering flames
R eptile family but they died.
O bviously clumsy but full of fun and hisses.
G reat at fighting.

Benjamin Britten (8)
Alver Valley Schools, Rowner

All About Fishrabbit

F ish is as strong as a shark.

I ncredible like a superhero.

S cary like a killer shark.

H ard like a gigantic rock.

R abbit is as fast as a cheetah.

A mazing but when he sees fish, he kills them.

B right like the blue breathtaking sea.

B oats are not stronger than my pet.

I love this pet because he is strong,

T idy and when he's angry, he eats fish instead of snakes.

Eric Gomes (9)

Alver Valley Schools, Rowner

Tiglion

T in is my pet, my pet, she just loves playing with tin.

I love my pet because she is very precious, pretty and very delicate like a flower.

G reat is my pet, that is true, she is an angel.

L ovely is my pet, she is like the moon.

I ncredible at catching prey because she is amazing at blending in.

O dd colours on her back, it is so she can blend in.

N othing can scare her because her ears are soundproof.

Ailish Richards (8)
Alver Valley Schools, Rowner

Cute Little Flippercorn

F antastic, fragile, freckly
L ush, loving heart
I ntelligent, intense body
P retty, peculiar pet
P etite, peticular vet
E veryone loves to pet her
R apping and running
C uddly, cute, colossal
O rdinary, nocturnal animal
R eddens in front of boys
N asty when she plays with his toys

But she is still my friend
Till the end.

Darcie Smith (8)
Alver Valley Schools, Rowner

The Sassiest Snake

S uper at swimming
A nd amazing at work
S uper at making tea
S he also loves planting flowers in her garden
Y ou should have heard that she has a yellow house

S he was born twenty-one years ago
N ew hairstyles every week
A nd loves pizza for dinner and apple crumble for dessert
K atey is her BFF's name
E mily is her big sister's name.

Lily Hall (9)
Alver Valley Schools, Rowner

Orange Puss In Boots

P rofessional, petrifying, pinpointing everything
U nder disguise, fighting crime, unique and
amazing
S hiny, sharp swords
S neaky, silent strides

I nnocent inky black eyes
N aughty by nature

B ouncing brightly and boldly against boulders
O range fur
O dd sounds
T iny Tonka toys
S ilent but deadly.

William François Frost (9)
Alver Valley Schools, Rowner

Super Bunny And The Food Machine

Super Bunny has colourful wings
She likes to eat colourful things
Her favourite thing is chicken wings.
She is furry and like silk,
She likes to drink milk.
She has a belt around her waist like cotton,
She has goggles around her eyes like Minions.
She has tiny fluffy feet with tiny shoes.
Super Bunny has big round eyes like bubbles.
Super Bunny has little furry paws that are pink.

Ruby Pitfield (8)
Alver Valley Schools, Rowner

Dumbum's Day

Dumbum likes to eat meat
And he needs to be neat.
In the morning, Dumbum eats pies
And wears ties.
Dumbum is fluffy
And he is huffy.
Dumbum's legs
Become pegs
At night!
Dumbum has sharp claws
At night, his claws snore!
Dumbum's head is wet.
Dumbum doesn't like flies
But he likes pies!
Dumbum likes doodles
But he doesn't like noodles.

Madison Walker (8)
Alver Valley Schools, Rowner

Cycling Tortoise

T iny like a cute long centipede
O nly cycling tortoise ever seen in the universe
R ough and scaly like a green fierce crocodile
T ired all the time but never gives up
O h so sweaty but never finishes riding
I nside, never - always out on his bicycle
S assy, cute and smiley
E ven though he is very unique, he could be your best friend.

Lillie Jade Buchanan (8)
Alver Valley Schools, Rowner

All About Wall Climber

Likes acorns, chocolate and meat.
Wall Climber is fussy, with specific types of chocolate.
Runs up tall buildings.
Cool is my pet mostly.
Eats frozen, chewy meat.
Likes to be as sneaky as a secret spy agent.
It's a terrifying, pessimistic turtle spider.
Love is what my pet uses to make people his personal friends.
Likes spiders because they're his friends.

Aiden McAllister (8)
Alver Valley Schools, Rowner

All About Toast The Cat

Toast likes to eat toast
And for dinner, she likes to have roast
Toast likes to eat meat
And she likes to stomp her feet
For lunch, she eats pie
While looking at the sky.
Toast likes to drink milk
And her body is as soft as silk
Toast's eyes are as dark as night
But she doesn't want a fright
Toast has claws that leave marks on the floor.

Karley Morgan (8)
Alver Valley Schools, Rowner

A Catgiraffe

C olourful, crazy giraffe
A lways tripping up on his long crazy tail
T all, fat and clumsy
G iving me a laugh
I nteresting, crazy Catgiraffe
R ide on his big, hairy, fat back
A mazing Catgiraffe has a long neck
F unny, crazy Catgiraffe
F unky, big, fat Catgiraffe
E vil, big Catgiraffe.

Elsie Smethest (8)
Alver Valley Schools, Rowner

My Giraffe-Cat Spots

S ome things about my pet:

P ointy, smooth ears so he can hear everything at all times.

O ther things will annoy him, but that won't stop him doing anything.

T all like a towering castle and he likes that because he can see everything.

S ome more things about him: he's funny, he can sometimes be sad and he's a Giraffe-Cat.

Laila-Mae Lavin (8)
Alver Valley Schools, Rowner

Super Cat

S uper Cat, as fast as a flash
U ltimate rush, a flash
P owers are super
E vil villain like a really nasty friend
R ushing to be like the Flash, he's brilliant

C reepy, terrifying, ugly monster!
A ble to save a person's life
T ired from all of the running and saving people's lives.

Layton Duruy (8)

Alver Valley Schools, Rowner

The Donutcorn

D ark and deep in the ocean
O reos are the best for Donutcorn
N ever being rude, she loves her friends
U nhappy when she gets bullied
T all and talented
C orns are for Donutcorn and ice cream,
O range hair that she dyed
R unning is her exercise
N ice people give her crowns.

Scarlett Hedger (8)
Alver Valley Schools, Rowner

Ninjamouse's Life

Ninjamouse is a hero
American, saving people
Ninjamouse climbs from house to house
Great, right
Also, he can run as fast as a cheetah
And he can jump the highest
Rhendeslee, a villain, was chasing Ninjamouse
But he lost the villain
Most of the time, he does parkour
When his shift is over
Also, he's really fast.

Reggie Peart (8)
Alver Valley Schools, Rowner

Derek Jr

D erek Jr is my friend, he will be till the end
E ager for a friend, he is the best till the end
R ed is his favourite colour, no need to hiss
E legant when he comes to school
K illing all hate in your heart

J umping all around the field
R unning in your eyesight to keep him near.

Beay Edwards (9)
Alver Valley Schools, Rowner

Flying Rat Gary

Gary's wings are as bright as a light in the sky.
Gary's teeth are like coral reef.
Gary's teeth are sharp and deep.
Gary's head is as big as a shed.
Gary's tail is as big as a whale.
Gary snores and he grows paws.
Gary's fluffy like a bunny.
Gary's keen and not so mean.

Amelie Langan (8)
Alver Valley Schools, Rowner

All About Felecia The Alicorn

F abulous at drawing
E xtremely kind to her friends
L oves riding her bicycle under the summer sun
E ats chocolate cake for her job
C an fly high in the sky at night
I ncredibly good at drawing rare red unicorns
A nd her favourite food is pop pop popcorn!

Lilliana Nelson (9)
Alver Valley Schools, Rowner

My Bearded Dragon Charmander

C ute and scaly

H e has a long tail

A lways likes to swim

R eally small

M ight breathe fire

A lways naughty

N ever stops eating

D aytime is his favourite time

E very day, he eats salad

R eally hungry all the time.

Joseph Feeley (8)
Alver Valley Schools, Rowner

Tiny Terror

T errifying and tiny
I ndependence and instant
N ice and sometimes naughty
Y oung, yawning

T ired tourist
E specially excited
R oaring real
R attling
O vertaking all the fighters
R aging at enemies.

Noah Styan (8)
Alver Valley Schools, Rowner

Crossycorn

C heerful, childish, colourful horn
R ainbow, rude unicorn
O dd, obedient
S assy, shiny, soft
S himmery, spectacular tongue
Y oung, yellow
C ute, cuddly fur
O rdinary
R esponsible, rider
N asty, naughty.

Lucy Francis (8)
Alver Valley Schools, Rowner

Super Cat

Super Cat is cool,
He always goes to the pool.

He is so sweet,
He goes to Pete's.

He has gentle ears,
He loves to take beers.

Super Cat has super legs,
He uses them for running.

Super Cat is lazy,
He hangs out with Daisy.

Marcus Kwabena Mprah (8)
Alver Valley Schools, Rowner

The Adventures Of Ace The Bat Hound

A gile and amazing, Olympic member
C almly collects his dimes and medals
E xcellent like a trained dog

D ogs can act like an angry dad
O ddly, older than God
G reatest gangster, most super dog ever.

Ben Kershaw (8)

Alver Valley Schools, Rowner

Tom-Flyer

T o fly in the sky
O ut is my lie
M y cat will cry and lie

F lies high
L ikes pie
Y ou are up high
E xcellent, beautiful crown
R acing to catch a mouse.

Raluca Segarceanu (8)
Alver Valley Schools, Rowner

Phinicx

P eculiar, handsome pet
H ungry, angry parrot
I ncredible colours
N obody can see him anywhere
I ncredible powers that will stick you to walls!
C ute face
X -ray vision.

Harvey Matthews (8)
Alver Valley Schools, Rowner

Tela-Squid

T elekinesis
E vil
L oves water
A rch-enemy is Cyborg Squirrel

S teals water
Q uick
U nder the sea
I n his lair
D epressed.

Harrison Pearce (8)

Alver Valley Schools, Rowner

Super Dog

S uperhero
U p, up, up in the sky
P ets love him
E ats dog treats
R ides on other

D ogs sometimes
O utside to do PE
G oes to the park.

Ila Kaminski (8)
Alver Valley Schools, Rowner

Bob

D ogs are as fluffy as cotton candy.
O wners take care of their dogs.
G reat friends to have as they are playful and joyful.

My pet can do a backflip
On a ship!

Max Butler (8)

Alver Valley Schools, Rowner

Edie

Edie the cat sat on a hat
So he could dodge the baseball bat
The ball flew past
Remarkably fast
So the dog tried to chase the hog
But the dog was stuck in the bog.

Harley Allen (9)
Alver Valley Schools, Rowner

Bad Dog

Bad boy dog
Has feet like a monster
And his head is the same size as a lobster!

Bad boy dog
Likes to eat
And when he does, it's raw meat.

George Grimes (8)
Alver Valley Schools, Rowner

Astronaut Sloth

S leepy and cute
L azy and wild
O dd and really popular
T akes all of the food
H ides in his tree.

Penelope Hearn (8)

Alver Valley Schools, Rowner

Working Dog Catches Bad Guys

D angerous dog with superpowers
O h, awesome thing it is
G reat and seeing and catching thieves.

Edward Harvey (9)
Alver Valley Schools, Rowner

Worm

W iggly worm

O ut in dirt

R olls

M uddy worm.

Archie Farrel (8)

Alver Valley Schools, Rowner

My Teddy Giraffe 'Jeff'

I have a teddy giraffe named Jeff,
But he's no normal teddy.
When the light's out and the moon is pearl-white
And very bright,
My teddy giraffe Jeff
Starts to shine really bright!
Wings start to grow
And on his head appears a halo!
Then he starts to move
And then he grows longer
Until he's the size of the smallest baby giraffe ever!
He wakes me up
With a smile on his face
And turns around
To show a cloud full of grace!
I nod my head
And he puts me on his back
Then he takes me away
On the cloud on his back!
We fly high in the sky
Until we stopped and saw a shooting star

So we stopped and made a wish!
Back home we went
And he put me in bed.
Safe and sound I am
In my bed
Along with Jeff
With his very long neck.
In the morning, he's back to normal
And a new story to tell Mum
About our magnificent adventure.

Georgie Short (8)
Newton Bluecoat CE Primary School, Newton With Scales

The Pegacorn!

I love my pet
Because it's a Pegacorn!
It is a unicorn and a horse mixed together.
It's the only one in the world.
So I show off
Like really show off
Anybody sees me
I will show off.
I fly on my unicorn horse!
It is the best feeling ever.
Riding on a pale yellow, lavender-purple Pegacorn
It's just the best feeling ever
People think it's scary
But it's really not.
Nobody knows where she came from
Or how,
People said she's immortal.
People said she's the only one of her kind.
People said she is a hybrid.
Nobody knows and that's why I love her

Because she is special, cute,
Kind and colourful.

Isla Bradley (8)
Newton Bluecoat CE Primary School, Newton With Scales

A Murder Mystery

Every night,
My Shadow Giraffe Teddy comes to life.
Every night,
He assassinates people
But never *ever* gets caught
Because he can run as fast as Usain Bolt.
My giraffe never dies -
It flies into the midnight sky.
But it hasn't always been like this
My giraffe has had an accident before,
Another murderer shot my giraffe's leg
He fell from the sky
But he persevered to fly.
Sadly, his leg fell off
So I gave him a plastic leg.
My giraffe makes the biggest crime scene in the
world,
Even Boris Johnson has sent a search party out
To find the murderer.
It's a murder mystery!

Bobby Hastwell (8)
Newton Bluecoat CE Primary School, Newton With Scales

Flying Unidog

There is an extraordinary pet coming through,
That will make your imagination come true!
It's called a Flying Unidog,
It can see through the fog!
It has shiny wings,
As shiny as rings!
It can fly at noon
Up to the moon!
It even has glasses,
Now this has gone to the masses!
It's very clever
And if you're scared of falling, that'll be never!
As you know, I'll tell you again,
It can spread its wings, just like a hen!
It's quicker on ice
And can easily see mice!
It's very cute
But can't play the flute.
He's sometimes lazy
But can go crazy!

Isaac Wearden (8)
Newton Bluecoat CE Primary School, Newton With Scales

Ziz Popper

I have a pet called Ziz Popper.
At night, he makes very dark lightning
If you saw him, you would be scared.
So don't look up, unless you're a Viking.
Because he's always hungry, *do not* go near him
Or he will kill you with one bite!
He is neon orange and metallic green, you will not
like him.
He's very creepy and colourful, so stay away or you
will die.
His teeth are bright yellow, his feet are hairy
And his long green tummy is spiky.
If you look in its neon-blue eyes, you will die
And by one single bite
So don't go near him
Unless you're a superhero.

Jude Westgate (8)
Newton Bluecoat CE Primary School, Newton With Scales

A Full Moon Surprise

Every full moon
Something special will happen in the zoo
A Uniphant will appear before your eyes -
Have you ever seen one before?
I'm guessing not...
It's pink and blue and has a horn
and don't forget the wings!
The Uniphant dances with the stars,
In the moonlight it glows
And finds its way to the moon.
The Uniphant only eats human food
Or it won't eat *anything* at all!
It loves watermelon, melon,
Peanuts and cucumber.
Its enemy is a piece of chocolate.
Dun, dun, dun!

Millie Singleton (8)
Newton Bluecoat CE Primary School, Newton With Scales

The Cowmall's Tea

I've never seen something like this before
He's got a mat on his back
And he eats cats.
So beware of the Cowmall!
He sleeps in the day
Awake at night.
He hates people
He kills people.
He's got sharp teeth
He's ready to eat.
While he isn't eating,
A lazy grump he is being.
He goes to sleep
Without a peep
And he loves to snore.
He's as feisty as a bull
He's got a horn,
His hump is mud-brown
Eyes are rose-red
And horn stone-grey.
Everybody hates him!

Logan Salisbury (8)
Newton Bluecoat CE Primary School, Newton With Scales

Evil Dino Duck!

Today, I saw an Evil Dino Duck at the end of my
street!
I was so shocked!
I never ever thought that I would see an Evil Dino
Duck.
The Evil Dino Duck
Gigantic and sassy,
Ferocious and red and black.
This was actually amazing,
Like wow!
I really never thought this would happen
But it did!
Who would ever see an Evil Dino Duck?
Me!
I guess I will go home now.
Well, that was an adventure with an Evil Dino Duck
Technically not with it,
But yeah
So bye!

Lyla Fegan (8)
Newton Bluecoat CE Primary School, Newton With Scales

Dino

It's a spooky, scary, Dino skeleton!
It's the colour of grass
It comes out at night and tries to hunt you down
It will eat you if it catches you
Dead or alive!
it jumps out to kill you.
It's very spooky,

The baby Dino is cute
But not as cute as the Meerkat.
The Meerkat is adorable
As soon as you see it, you will fall in love
The other Dino is brown like a log.
They are cute on the outside
But not on the inside...

Paige Hulme (8)
Newton Bluecoat CE Primary School, Newton With Scales

The Liger's Life

Liger, Liger, Liger she is,
She lives in the middle of the jungle and also hunts her prey.
She doesn't eat people,
She's cute and adorable.
She doesn't bite,
She will only play.
She is the cutest thing you'll ever see
And her name is Ellie.
She hunts at night and only eats bugs,
And anyway, she won't bug you.
She is cute, as you know.
So have lots of fun!

Harriet Cross (8)
Newton Bluecoat CE Primary School, Newton With Scales

Squibin's Day At The Beach

Squibin's at the beach
Pecking at the pebbles,
Screeching loudly
Squawk!
Everybody got annoyed.
He mistook someone's foot as a pebble
And pecked their toe hard.
Ow!
Squibin flew away
Squawking to his owner
When he got locked in his cage.
Hours later
He got out
He broke out
Now he's living in the woods
Multiplying...

Alfie Jones (8)
Newton Bluecoat CE Primary School, Newton With Scales

The Gisplot's Day At Home

My marvellous pet is called the Gisplot.
It is very cool
It eats stones
So you never have to feed it.
There is only one problem
He can't sit in my home
So he sleeps on the grass.
It has gills that don't work
So they are useless!
It's yellow
It's breathtaking
It is like the sun, or better!
Every night, we fly to the moon
Just us, together.

Ben Bayley (8)
Newton Bluecoat CE Primary School, Newton With Scales

Breakdancing Guinea Pig

At night, my guinea pig does a dance,
He jumps, he spins, he does a little prance.
He rolls down the steps onto the mat,
He rolls through the cat flap and he sees a rat.
He spins on his head and gets really dizzy,
So he goes all whizzy.
He jumps, he spins, he whirls around,
He goes faster than the speed of sound!

Amelia Cole (9)
Newton Bluecoat CE Primary School, Newton With Scales

Wolf Trap

He liked rainbow stuff
Like rainbow squishy toys
And rainbow bikes
There was a secret place underground
It was full of rainbow stuff
There were rainbow bikes
Rainbow lamps
Rainbow iPads and Nintendos
But there was one more thing...
Rainbow chocolates
Rainbow chocolate eggs!

Alijah Davidson (8)
Newton Bluecoat CE Primary School, Newton With Scales

The Half Angel Half Devil

It's red like a devil.
It's blue like the ocean.
It's purple like an English book.
He is the size of two buildings.
He can do anything you want.
His claws are as sharp as a knife.
Dino Wings is stronger than a bull.
He can knock down a building with one punch!

Xzavier Whitehead (8)
Newton Bluecoat CE Primary School, Newton With Scales

Ploth

I got a teddy from a shop.
I put it on my bed.
I got up in the night
And rubbed my head.
It had wings and could fly
High to the sky!
The face is brown
And he is flying round the town.
He flies higher and higher
Breathing fire and more fire!

Zak Tabbenor (9)
Newton Bluecoat CE Primary School, Newton With Scales

The Flying Uni-Ale

Once, in the sea,
There was a Uni-Ale who liked to eat pink peas
In the night, he learned to fly with me -
He went so high,
Higher than a fly
That buzzes around so much in the sky.
My Uni-Ale is sparkly
It is colourful
And it's mine.

Joshua Baugh (8)
Newton Bluecoat CE Primary School, Newton With Scales

See Mouse

S ees in the dark

E xpands

E xchanger

M illions of mice in the world

O utside mouse

U se him for a mouse spy

S kinny mouse

E xtra sticky!

Scott Simpson (8)

Newton Bluecoat CE Primary School, Newton With Scales

Silly Billy Bill

S illy Billy Bill is very clumsy.

I am Shyloh and I am gonna introduce him.

L amb is his favourite food.

L oving me all day.

Y ellow is his favourite colour because he is yellow.

B ill has a top-hat beetle, he is yellow and he has one eye, black arms and black legs and he's clumsy.

I love him so much.

L ove him, he's a special clumsy pet.

L ooney Tune he's a bit like.

Y ellow is his friend.

B ill is the best.

I will feed him.

L et's feed him some dog food.

L icking, licking and licking the food, I love him.

Shyloh Gould (7)
St Joseph's & St Gregory's Catholic Primary School, Biddenham

Cute Cats

Cute cats fly over the sky
Every morning, afternoon and night
Oh, Rainbow
Oh, Rainbow
Come and eat your colourful food
Rainbow gobbled his food
Next, the adorable Rainbow saw the moon outside
Rainbow's eyes glowed
Rainbow flew over the moon
She flies as light as a feather
The next morning, the cat was magical
Rainbow flew and gave food to her children
Rainbow's owner said to Rainbow,
"Oh Rainbow dear, come here
You are very kind, caring
You give charity every single day
Give food to your children
I can't believe it."

Aleeza Hayat (7)

St Joseph's & St Gregory's Catholic Primary School,
Biddenham

My Peculiar Pet

Soon, in the farm, my ugly giraffe poops, every day.
On Monday, he pooped on people's heads.
On Tuesday, he did the same.
On Wednesday, he did it again!
Kangaroo came and said, "You should not poo on people's heads!
Your poo is disgusting, why do you poo all the time?"
"Because that's my job."
He is peculiar.
He is serious.
"Next time, Giraffe, never do it again."
"I promise!" he said.

Anna Olutimayin (6)
St Joseph's & St Gregory's Catholic Primary School, Biddenham

My Peculiar Pet

"Fear me, I am a dangerous puppy."
Eats food which is adult food.
Lazy and it plays all day long.
After it pops in the toilet, off it pops outside.
Dog that pops every day.
Oh, and it bites.
Good dog and I love him.
Pops in my bedroom.
Oh, and it pops while it's skipping.
Lazy dog always
But it saves everyone.
Eats dog food as well.
So we called him Super Pup.
Eats eggs.

Michael Udoh (6)
St Joseph's & St Gregory's Catholic Primary School,
Biddenham

Lilana Is Flying In The Sky For Once

L ilana is magical and fun
I t is amazing that she can fly
L ots of people need her
A nimals should get so much love
N o animal should suffer
A nd especially not Lilana.

Look at the pretty little kitty
Gnawing on her bone
How I wish she'd eat some fish
And leave my leg alone!
She is never going to go on her own.

Apio Okel (8)
St Joseph's & St Gregory's Catholic Primary School,
Biddenham

Shell Koala

S he had to slither all over the place.

H er shell was peach.

E veryone was playing with her.

L ooking at her.

L iked her.

K ittens played with the Shell Koala.

O cean was her favourite thing.

A kitten was playing.

L iked kittens.

A cat pounced on her.

Jake Palmer (6)

St Joseph's & St Gregory's Catholic Primary School,
Biddenham

Mr Prawl

Mr Prawl,
A creepy crawl,
With a frivolous mane,
As he creeps up and down the lane.
He lives in a cave
As dangerous as a dark, gloomy grave.
Can you crawl over a rainbow
As it gives a bright glow?
You prowl so quiet and slow,
That the only sound is the breeze's blow.
Your voice is the greatest I know!

Aradhana James (8)
St Joseph's & St Gregory's Catholic Primary School,
Biddenham

My Fantastic Pet

My dog is really bad
In the night, he barks
In the morning, he's asleep
He's a robot
And is mad and hard.
My dog's name is Lion
He likes to bite as well.
He scratches with sharp metal claws.
He's really colourful
And has all the colours painted on the metal.
He scratches like chalk.

Mason Grygiel-Smith (6)
St Joseph's & St Gregory's Catholic Primary School,
Biddenham

Pakaroo

P akaroo is my pet.

A t the park, Pakaroo loves playing with me.

K ittens are scared of Pakaroo.

A t home, me and Pakaroo love playing with my toys.

R adishes are Pakaroo's favourite food.

O wlpus is Pakaroo's friend.

O cean is Pakaroo's favourite.

Jihan Alom (6)

St Joseph's & St Gregory's Catholic Primary School, Biddenham

Duckfly

D uckfly is my pet.
U p she flaps her wings in the sky.
C arrot is her favourite food.
K ittens try to chase her.
F luttering feather friend.
L ove to have a pink and yellow pet.
Y ou love your Duckfly!

Mahdiya Bi (7)
St Joseph's & St Gregory's Catholic Primary School,
Biddenham

Rockabean

Once, under a bench, there was a rock
Who lived quite close to the sea.
People called him an amazing name,
It was Rockabean!
Rockabean was good!
Rockabean liked food!
Rockabean is so good
You'll want him so bad!

Breann D'souza (6)
St Joseph's & St Gregory's Catholic Primary School,
Biddenham

Flying Cat

I have a pet
His name is Fluffy
When it's daytime
She is a normal cat
But when it's night-time
She is flying cat!
With her sparkly wings
She can fly all the way to the moon
And that is Fluffy
My flying cat.

Grazi Alexandre Cardoso (7)
St Joseph's & St Gregory's Catholic Primary School,
Biddenham

The Hero Dog Saves The Day!

This is a poem about a hero dog
Roses are red
Dogs can fly
But not every dog!
Only this dog can fly
I know it's crazy
But this dog will save the day
A building was burning
Hero Dog went and saved the people.

Marcel Popko (7)

St Joseph's & St Gregory's Catholic Primary School,
Biddenham

Timathy The Turtle

T imathy the amazing turtle

"I 'm very slimy."

M arvellous Timmy

A mazing to play with

T imathy the incredible

H e is very cute

Y ou will be happy with him.

Arman Chimber (8)

St Joseph's & St Gregory's Catholic Primary School,
Biddenham

Jongy The Cat

J ongy the cute cat

O h, Jongy loves oranges.

"N o!" I tell him not to spit. "That is not good."

G ood Jongy because he was a good boy.

Y ellow is his favourite colour.

Aaminah Khan (7)

St Joseph's & St Gregory's Catholic Primary School,
Biddenham

Owlpus

O wlpus' favourite food is strawberries.

W ater she likes to hang out in.

L et the Owlpus out of the ocean.

P arrots like to chase Owlpus.

U nder the sea.

S ea creature.

Vilte Zubaviciute (6)

St Joseph's & St Gregory's Catholic Primary School, Biddenham

Octerou

O cter is my pet.
C arrot is its favourite food.
T rees can be destroyed
E ats seahorses.
R uns around the sea
O wls are its enemy
U nderwater is its favourite.

Mujtabah Shahab (7)

St Joseph's & St Gregory's Catholic Primary School,
Biddenham

Bob The Cat

G igantic Bob the lazy, clever snake.

R unning, fast legs.

U nhappy mood.

M essy, wild wings when he flies.

P ain is his weakness.

Y ellow is his favourite colour.

Enzo Bucolo (7)

St Joseph's & St Gregory's Catholic Primary School, Biddenham

Tiger

The tiger was hunting
His name was Flow
He went to look for people
His eyes were orange
His tongue was black
He had purple spots on his back
He found a human
He ate it
All gobbled up!

Hafsa Mahmood (7)
St Joseph's & St Gregory's Catholic Primary School,
Biddenham

Duckfly

D uckfly is my pet
U p it goes.
C arrots are its favourite food.
K ittens eat them!
F eather friends
L ove to play
Y ou are my best friend.

Imogen Waruhari (6)

St Joseph's & St Gregory's Catholic Primary School,
Biddenham

Owpus

O wpus is my favourite pet.
W aves she likes.
P at is her friend.
U p - she thinks about outside.
S he loves to eat carrots and peas, even caramel.

Rameesha Begum (6)

St Joseph's & St Gregory's Catholic Primary School,
Biddenham

Catdog

C atdog is my pet.

A lways eats my newspaper.

T iny is Catdog.

D angerous is Catdog.

O nly he is special.

G old is special to Catdog.

Nihal Gill (6)

St Joseph's & St Gregory's Catholic Primary School, Biddenham

Super Wulfy The Dog

W ulfy was wearing some spots.
U ngrateful, useless and undeciding.
L azy, little, lonely Wulfy.
F uzzy, frightening dog.
Y elling, young dog.

Achan Okel (8)

St Joseph's & St Gregory's Catholic Primary School,
Biddenham

Little Lilli The Cat

L illi the cat

I ncredible cat always

L ittle cat, small cat

L azy and messy all the time

I mprover every time.

Ellis Matarazzo (7)

St Joseph's & St Gregory's Catholic Primary School, Biddenham

Lily The Highlight Kitty Lion

L ittle, tiny lion!
I ncredible cheeky lion
L ion in the wild!
Y es, the best Highlight Kitty Lion.

Nimrah Iqbal (7)

St Joseph's & St Gregory's Catholic Primary School, Biddenham

Giraffisor

This is my pet
It has peculiar feathers
Giraffe
Bee tail
Horse legs
Rabbit eyes
My peculiar giraffe.

Manha Farheen (6)

St Joseph's & St Gregory's Catholic Primary School,
Biddenham

Tim The Fish

T im the super fish.

"I can be dangerous."

M y fishes - that one of them is bad.

Rizwan Waheed (7)

St Joseph's & St Gregory's Catholic Primary School,
Biddenham

The Amazing Swag

S wag is a spectacular, fashionable pet

W onderful pet! He's as swag as a rich man

A n outstanding swaggy pet, responsible as a dog

G etting up is very tricky

F unny as a clown on a comedian stage

A s excited as a frog, he's a very funny dog

S waggy as John Cena, his tail swings at the enemy

H appy like a child looking at its first rainbow

I ncredible ideas for fashion, but his ideas go overboard

O n Sundays, he sleeps in for fifteen hours!

N ever gives up on a fashion idea

I ncredibly funny on Saturdays but very serious on Wednesdays

S adly, he has a small family but he has me

T oo funny, I can hardly talk

A ll other times, he likes to sit out in the sun with some dog food.

Deja Parker (10)

St Palladius Primary School, Dalry

Artie The Annoying Armadillo

A rtie the Annoying Armadillo is one of the most annoying pets

R anting on and on about apples

T oday, he ate 11,000,001 apples, that's a new record!

I n Artie's room, you will find him surrounded by an apple wonderland

E nchanting, semi-strange features include: chin hair, bright cyan colour handle-bar moustache, lipstick, Peppa Pig high heels, a camel hump, a fluffy ballpoint tail and lots more

A lmond Weetabix with apple shavings on top is his dream breakfast

R ed-coloured things he will eat in a heartbeat, so make sure not to have any red clothes on if you see him!

M aybe he might join the circus because he is incredible at balancing on things.

A fter he joins the circus, maybe he will make friends with a purple bear called Jacob.

D own underground is where he was born, the lack of oxygen is what gave him his bright cyan colour. As for the other things... well, let's just say eating too many apples does stuff to you!

I n the woods you would never find him, so don't bother looking in there if he ever goes missing

L oud and obnoxious is how his voice sounds

L evitation is key if anything red surrounds you

O verall, he's a pretty annoying pet but I wouldn't trade him in the world.

Emma Galloway (11)
St Palladius Primary School, Dalry

Sticky

S ticky is the most strangest pet known,
T he hardest job is feeding,
I t takes fourteen bags of rice to make him full!
C arrying him is like holding a massive ball of hair,
K icking makes Sticky tired in no time.
Y ears after owning him, he is ready for another owner

T his does get stressful after a while, nevertheless,
H e is very friendly (sometimes...) with his Kim K lipstick,
E yeshadow is the key to trust Sticky (shout out to James Charles)

C utting his hair is very scary for Sticky (he needs a wig)
H aving Sticky is like a living make-up pallet,
I n Sticky's room, you will be greeted with a picture of Kim K,
L oving Sticky is very simple, so come on round for a Sticky,
L iving with Sticky is very hard at times, but
I think you should give Sticky a try! (Good luck...)

Skye McDowall (11)
St Palladius Primary School, Dalry

Brilliant Spy Cat

B rilliant, skilled Spy Cat is special

R eady to do anything any day

I t lives in a warm, cosy cat tower

L ate at night, thieves never get away because Spy Cat spots them

L ost cats always try to play with the incredible Spy Cat of town

I t is very easy for Spy Cat to use some of her spy gadgets

A dorable Spy Cat gets all the attention from everyone

N ever has she been able to use her laser pen and now she can

T iny Spy Cat wears a colourful mask on her face

S assy Spy Cat walks around, feeling happy all day

P eaceful days are good for Spy Cat so she can relax all day

Y ou can see her chilling next to the pool

C lever Spy Cat finished another mission again
A ll the cats are so proud of her
T hen everything she got and she was happy.

Lucy Allan (11)
St Palladius Primary School, Dalry

My Pet Centaurogaf

C entaurogaf is an endangered creature
E very other Centaurogaf is probably dead
N ormal intelligence but mighty strength
T alented as an athlete but as clumsy as a comedian
A s fast as the sewage and as smart as a high-school beginner
U nder the weather most of the time
R unning right to me, the first time we've seen each other
O n Sunday, it jogs around the garden
G etting food for it feels almost impossible
A fter four weeks of having it, I thought it would be extinct
F unny, it sleeps too much.

Ivie James Sharp (10)
St Palladius Primary School, Dalry

Robbin The Bird

R obbin loves to fly
O ver towns and cities
B lue are her feathers, with
B eautiful dark eyes
I ncredibly fast when she flies
N ever stop Robbin because she can bite

T hough it is unusual, because she is friendly
H ome she flies to after a long day
E very day, she's stealing food

B ut, at night, she's innocent
I ncredibly fast, she ran into someone
R ight away, she knew she wasn't safe
D espises being in front of a human, she flew as
fast as ever.

Caoilin O'Reilly (9)
St Palladius Primary School, Dalry

Bob The Warrior Fish

B ob is a warrior fish
O range skin and a purple hat
B ig and bold

T all as a giraffe
H e likes to fight the chip shop man
E very night

W atch out
A lways fast
R eally sneaky
R ight on time
I nside the chip shop he sneaks
O ut of nowhere, he appears
R unning towards the chip shop

F ight, fight, fight!
I n the night
S lapping Mr Chip Shop Man with
H addock to the face - bash!

Cameron Irvine (10)
St Palladius Primary School, Dalry

Dot The Turtle

D ot the turtle is very scared of humans

O range dots are a part of my turtle

T he turtle is very rare

T he turtle is very smart

H e likes to swim each day

E ach day, Dot the turtle always swims the deepest water

T he turtle is very, very smart about the sea

U nder the water, he can see and breathe

R eally deep he can swim

T urtles can go deeper and deeper if they want

L aughing under the water

E ating vegetables under the water.

Kahlan Parker (10)

St Palladius Primary School, Dalry

Patch The Cat

P atch is a black and white kitten

A nd, at night, he is superhero.

T he toy I got him, a new toy, he loves to be

C heeky when I am annoyed at him

H e always like to try and sneak out.

T he cat called Patch is such a fool sometimes

H e loves to get comfy

E ach night with me, my cat likes to get comfy

C at loves to go out but fails the test

A t dinnertime, when I have fish and chips, he steals my fish!

T he cat loves to play with me.

Hayden McKerrell (8)
St Palladius Primary School, Dalry

Bolt The Dragon

B olt the dragon is superb

O ther people are scared of Bolt

L azy Bolt likes to sleep and be very lazy

T ame with his baby friends

T he dragon breathes roasting fire

H appy as a smiley emoji

E njoys playing in the forest

D ucking and diving in the sky

R eaching the clouds above

A fterwards, sleeps under the stars

G roaning and snoring

O ver the hills

N ow he sees two people from school.

Robert O'Pray (11)
St Palladius Primary School, Dalry

Fishy Frank

F ishy Frank loves to recycle. He
I s stinky like rotten tuna and
S illy like a pufferfish too.
H is family love him like a Cuddlefish
Y ou should too!

F ishy Frank hates the land because of littering
"R ecycle to save me and my family please!" he
cries
"A nd don't litter because you might go to jail
N ever litter, I'm warning you!
K ing Fishy might attack you, so don't litter!"

Archie Eagleson (8)

St Palladius Primary School, Dalry

The Crazy Man

Bartman is a raptor
He is the only one of his species
He is a bit crazy
Because he runs into danger
And defeats the criminals
But not always does he win
He lives in Scotland
In the closets of Dulry
He's a bit like Santa
He knows when a criminal is striking
He knows where it is as well.
He has no owner
The evillest villain in the world, Doctor James
Always kills
He wants to destroy the world...

A J Logan (9)
St Palladius Primary School, Dalry

Bolt The Dog

B olt the dog is super and he likes treats
O ver the roofs you'll see him running,
L eaping and jumping
T o save people and animals from things

T he dog is an Albino, as white as snow
H e is as fast as lightning
E ats energy dog snacks

D istracts his enemies with his boomerang bone
O ut every day, saving everyone
G igantic speed of Bolt the dog.

Cole Barclay (10)
St Palladius Primary School, Dalry

Banjo And Kazooie

B anjo and Kazooie are hyper all the time!
A s clever as can be
N ot bad at all
J aunty as a buzzing bee
O pposite of boring

K een to help Banjo out
A ware of bad guys
Z ooming through the sky
O utstanding flying skills
O ptimistic, just like Banjo
I nteresting feathers, look like a sunset
E pic adventures they have together!

Dale McCann (10)
St Palladius Primary School, Dalry

Chi The Panda

C hi saves China. She is a ninja panda.
H elping China during wars and fights.
I ntelligent and smart

T he panda is always willing and
H appy to help China.
E xercises to keep strong!

P atches are black and white
A perfect friend.
N ever leaves your sight.
D on't go on without her
A n amazing helper!

Hannah Krishnamuthe (10)
St Palladius Primary School, Dalry

Nugget The Noble

Nugget the Noble is very unique
She goes around every day of the week.
Every night, her cage lifts up and away she goes
She eats and sleeps all day long and then she gets into her clothes.
She flies far and close
She flies out of the window
Nugget gets all the info and helps other animals who need help
She puts on her magic belt
Nugget the Noble is very unique.

Lucy McCallum (11)
St Palladius Primary School, Dalry

Roger Racoon

R oger loves to play football
O verly fast
G oals all the time
E very game he wins
R eally good player

R unning with the ball
A lways on the treadmill, training
C an jump as high as a tall building
O ver the other players
O pposition has a chance
N ext day, he won a trophy.

Andrew Fraser (9)
St Palladius Primary School, Dalry

Sam The Super Snail

Sam the Super Snail loves to save people
From all different dangers.
His favourite food is dragon fruit.
It gives him a lot of energy.
He has a job as a model.
Every month, he slithers down the red carpet.

The reason Sam has another job
Is because sometimes there isn't anybody to save!
Other than that, he slithers down the runway
In style.

Maisy Berrie (9)
St Palladius Primary School, Dalry

Amy The Cat

A my is nice and sweet
M um takes Amy to Animal School
Y esterday, she went with her friend

T oday, she's going to Sunny Joe's
H er friend won a certificate
E very day, she waits for her friend

C onstantly talks to Mia
A ll the time
T omorrow, it's the holidays!

Jodie Thompson (8)
St Palladius Primary School, Dalry

Death Fury Dragon

D eath Fury
E ats anything in sight
A lways wins battles
T he teeth are loud like thunder drums
H e is faster than a speedy stinger

F erociously hunts
U nbelievable, humongous
R oars so loud, he rattles the sky
Y ou won't want to mess with the Death Fury
Dragon.

Max Livingstone (9)
St Palladius Primary School, Dalry

Bob Fishy

B ob Fishy is an arty fish
O h and he is ten years old
B ut in fish years, he is actually twenty

F ishy - middle name, Bob Fishy
I ncredibly talented, his art costs £100
S ure, it cost a couple of pounds
H e is a scarer but he is clever
Y ou can be his friend.

Riley Doak Winton (9)
St Palladius Primary School, Dalry

144

Pete The Powerful Panda

Pete is a very powerful panda
Who likes to eat his feet!
He is very cute
And is obsessed with his foot.
He likes to eat corn
And has a hidden horn.
Pete was born in the middle of the Arctic ocean
Being fully warm
And holding corn.
He got made jagged by a thorn
Which gave him magic powers.

Alan Billy Lee Harkins (10)
St Palladius Primary School, Dalry

Georgia The Guinea Pig

Georgia the guinea pig is very, very small.
She has four little legs
And crawls about the floor.
She always wears a bright green top
And likes to play with bouncy balls.
But when no one's watching
She will prepare for take-off,
Flap her wings and fly out the door.

Grace Wright (9)
St Palladius Primary School, Dalry

Catcorn

C atcorn is a very lazy pet

A lways adorable and cute

T ame and cuddly, she lies on the couch

C lever and colourful

O ver the fields she flies

R eally enjoys playing with children

N ever complains, Catcorn is the best peculiar pet.

Danielle Kilday (11)

St Palladius Primary School, Dalry

Zebedy Zebra

Z ebedy Zebra is a zesty pet.

E xcited as a person at Christmas

B ecause of all the cartwheels she can do

E xtraordinary Zebra does the splits

D ancing, dedicated to the music

Y ou are amazed at Zebedy Zebra's gymnastic moves.

Destiny Allan (11)
St Palladius Primary School, Dalry

Bobbi Tarantula

Bobbi the big tarantula
Drives a school bus
The children are scared of her
But don't make a fuss.
Bobbi loves the children
They make her laugh and smile
She wishes the children would talk to her
Once in a while.

Tilly Murdoch (9)
St Palladius Primary School, Dalry

YOUNG wRITERS INFORMATION

We hope you have enjoyed reading this book – and that you will continue to in the coming years.

If you're a young writer who enjoys reading and creative writing, or the parent of an enthusiastic poet or story writer, do visit our website **www.youngwriters.co.uk**. Here you will find free competitions, workshops and games, as well as recommended reads, a poetry glossary and our blog. There's lots to keep budding writers motivated to write!

If you would like to order further copies of this book, or any of our other titles, then please give us a call or order via your online account.

Young Writers
Remus House
Coltsfoot Drive
Peterborough
PE2 9BF
(01733) 890066
info@youngwriters.co.uk

Join in the conversation!
Tips, news, giveaways and much more!

 YoungWritersUK

 @YoungWritersCW